CEUTA
Mini Guide

Hugh George Griffin

Copyright © 2010
Savanna Press

www.savannapress.com

British Library Cataloguing-in-Publication Data

A catalogue record for this book is available from the British Library

ISBN: 978-0-9543335-3-9

All rights reserved. No part of this publication may be reproduced, stored in a retrieval system, or transmitted, in any form or by any means, electronic, mechanical, photocopying, recording or otherwise, without the prior permission of the publisher.

Credits:
The photographs in this book were supplied by Annette Griffin.

CONTENTS

Introduction	4
A Brief History	5
Getting There	6
Accommodation	8
Eating Out	9
Shopping	10
Sightseeing	11
• The Royal Walls	11
• *Parque Marítimo*	12
• Statues and Sculptures	12
• Arabic Baths	13
• *Fortaleza del Hacho*	13
• *Mirador de San Antonio*	13
• *Palacio Municipal*	14
• Ceuta Cathedral	14
• *Nuestra Señora de África*	14
• Mosque of *Sidi Embarek*	14
• Synagogue of *Bet-El*	15
Museums	15
• Ceuta Museum	15
• Museum of the Royal Walls	15
• *Exposición César Manrique*	15
• Military Museum	15
• Museum of the Legion	16
• Army Museum	16
• Maritime Museum	16
• Cathedral Museum	16
• Basilica Museum	16

Beaches	17
• *La Ribera*	17
• *El Chorrillo*	17
• *Playa Benítez*	17
• *Playa de Benzú*	17
Sports and Activities	18
• Kayak Hire	18
• Horse Riding	18
• *Club Náutico*	18
• Scuba Diving	18
• Hill Walking	18
• Motor Sports	18
• Fishing	19
Fiestas and Events	19
• *Los Reyes Magos*	19
• Ceuta Carnival	19
• Easter and Holy Week	19
• May Crosses	19
• *Corpus Christi*	19
• *Romería de San Antonio*	19
• *Nuestra Señora del Carmen*	20
• *Hogueras de San Juan*	20
• *Fiestas Patronales*	20
• Ceuta Day	20
• *San Daniel*	20
• Rucksack Day	21
Excursions	21
• Excursion to Gibraltar	21
• Excursion to Tetuan	23
Ceuta Facts and Figures	26
Hints and Tips	26
Useful Web Sites	27
Feedback Request	28

Las Murallas Reales protected Ceuta from attack for hundreds of years.

INTRODUCTION

Ceuta is a quirky and exotic part of Spain located in the African continent sharing a land border with Morocco and enjoying a Mediterranean shoreline and climate. The city sits at the gateway between the Mediterranean Sea and the Atlantic Ocean, links the continents of Europe and Africa and is a meeting point of four cultures and religions. From here you can see two continents and three countries: Great Britain (Gibraltar), Spain and Morocco. Although only about 23 square kilometres in size and with a population of just under 80,000, Ceuta comprises a harmonious mixture of cultures and religions including Christians, Muslims, Hindus and Jews. Monte Hacho, the low mountain in Ceuta, is claimed as one of the mythological Pillars of Hercules, the other being Gibraltar on the European side of the Mediterranean.

Referred to as the "Autonomous City of Ceuta", this Spanish enclave is an integral part of the Spanish state and is therefore part of the territory of the European Union. The Spanish Legion (formerly known as the Spanish Foreign Legion) has a garrison here. The Spanish and EU flags are flown on public buildings, the official language is Spanish and the euro is the official currency.

Ceuta is steeped in history and contains several ancient monuments, a number of museums and a varied architecture. The city also boasts sandy Mediterranean beaches and a pleasant climate. Due to its special low-tax status, prices of many goods are lower than in mainland Spain while the more energetic visitors have a choice of water sports, scuba diving or mountain trekking. The Mediterranean Maritime Park is one of the main tourist attractions with artificial lakes and formal gardens.

The city offers a choice of hotels from the four star Parador Hotel to budget priced hostels and guesthouses. There is a wide range of restaurants, predominantly Spanish and Moroccan but also many others varieties including Chinese, pizza and burger restaurants.

This fascinating city is easily reached by a frequent ferry service from Algeciras in southern Spain or a 30-minute helicopter journey from Málaga. Ceuta is an ideal destination for a day-trip as part of a holiday in the Costa del Sol but a longer stay is recommended in order to enjoy fully this charming piece of Europe on the African continent.

Murals depicting ancient scenes and scripts can be found around the city.

A BRIEF HISTORY

Recent archaeological discoveries have indicated that people have lived in this region since the Paleolithic era. Over the ages the area has been populated at various times by the Carthaginians, Romans, Vandals, Byzantines, Visigoths and Arabs. During the Middle Ages Ceuta became an important trading centre for European merchants and in 1415 the Portuguese took control under the leadership of John I of Portugal. At this time the pope conferred it with the title of "city". During subsequent decades Ceuta gained the institutions and appearance of a European city. The king of Spain seized the Portuguese throne in 1580 and held it for 60 years. During this time Ceuta gained many residents of Spanish origin.

A treaty between Spain and Portugal in 1668 led to Ceuta coming under Spanish control again and the city gained a Statute of Autonomy. The 18th and 19th centuries saw many new arrivals to Ceuta, in particular South American exiles, many of whom played an important role in the development of the city.

The African War (also known as the Spanish-Moroccan War) of 1859-60 began with a dispute over the borders of the city and was fought in northern Morocco. A Spanish victory was achieved following the Battle of Tetuan.

The Spanish Protectorate of Morocco, known simply as Spanish Morocco and encompassing much of northern Morocco, was established in 1912 and had its capital in Tetuan. Ceuta was not included as it was considered an integral part of the Spanish state. Spain recognized the independence of Spanish Morocco in 1956 but Ceuta and the other Spanish enclave of Melilla remained under Spanish rule.

In July 1936, General Francisco Franco took command of the Spanish Army in Africa and rebelled against the Spanish republican government in a military uprising that was to lead to the Spanish Civil War. The troops were transported to mainland Spain in an airlift using transport aircraft supplied by Germany and Italy. Ceuta was one of the first casualties of

A view along the *Calle Independencia* with Ceuta cathedral on the left and a glimpse of *Playa de la Ribera* to the right.

Statue of a religious figure in the *Calle Camoens*.

Ships in the Strait of Gibraltar between Algeciras and Ceuta.

the uprising. The citizens of Ceuta were repressed by the rebel nationalist forces led by General Franco while at the same time the city came under fire from the air and sea forces of the republican government.

During the fascist years Ceuta built on its reputation as a trading post. Following the death of General Franco and the restoration of democracy, Ceuta had its Statute of Autonomy restored, albeit not until 1995. Modern Ceuta benefits from investment and funding from the Spanish government and the European Union. It is a cosmopolitan city with a significant Berber Muslim community as well as Sephardic Jewish and Hindu minorities.

GETTING THERE

The only land border is with Morocco. If you are coming from Morocco you can cross the border at Tarajal either by car or on foot. Neither buses nor taxis cross the border so if you do not have your own transport it is necessary to take a taxi to the border on the Moroccan side and walk through to the Spanish side. There are various passport checks and customs formalities, both Moroccan and Spanish, and you will need a valid passport. If you are not a citizen of the EU you may also need a visa. Once on the Spanish side go to the bus stop on the right hand side of the road about 100 metres from the frontier. Bus number 7 will take you to the city centre for less than a euro. The buses are frequent and you should not have to wait more than ten to fifteen minutes. The trip takes about fifteen minutes and you should ask for the *Plaza de la Constitución*. The bus stops on the street outside the covered market, *el Mercado Central*.

Mural depicting an ancient scene in Ceuta.

Ceuta does not have an airport but it does have a heliport. There are several helicopter flights every day between Ceuta and Málaga in southern Spain. This route is operated by Inaer (http://www.grupoinaer.com/index.php?/inaer/malagaceuta Tel. +00 34 902 101 697) and tickets cost around 140 euros for a single journey. You can book online at eDreams (http://www.edreams.com/flights/malaga-ceuta). The flight takes about 35 minutes and affords excellent views of the

Strait of Gibraltar. Flights leave Málaga from the international airport. In Ceuta, the heliport is a ten to fifteen minute walk to the centre. If you are travelling by air to Málaga, the helicopter route is a convenient connection to Ceuta. Málaga is served by many scheduled and charter flights.

Ceuta can be reached by ferry from Algeciras on the southern tip of Spain. There are frequent fast ferries run by several companies including AccionaTransmediterranea (http://www.trasmediterranea.es), Euroferrys (http://www.euroferrys.com) and Balearia (http://www.balearia.com). The crossing takes less than an hour and single tickets cost around 30 euros for foot passengers. You can bring your car for around 100 euros. Tickets can be booked online in advance but generally this is not necessary and you can buy your ticket at the port or in many travel agencies in the vicinity. Arriving at the ferry terminal in Algeciras is best done by taxi as it is a large port and you can easily go to the wrong terminal. Tell your driver that you are getting a boat to Ceuta so he knows where to take you. The ferries for Ceuta share a terminal building with the ferries for Tanger (Tangiers). Once at the terminal you will need to exchange your ticket for a boarding card and then proceed through security.

The Mediterranean Sea from Ceuta.

The ferry journey is fast and comfortable and affords excellent views of the Rock of Gibraltar and the coasts of both African and Europe. There are snack bars and shops at the terminal and on board the ferry.

Algeciras can be reached by train or bus. Fast trains from Madrid take approximately four hours. There is a Spanish National Railways, or Renfe, office (http://www.renfe.es or http://www.spanish-rail.co.uk) in Ceuta in the *Plaza Rafael Gibert*, a few minutes from the *Plaza de la Constitución*, should you need to buy tickets for mainland Spain. Buses go to Algeciras from various cities in southern Spain including Granada, Fuengirola, Almería, Marbella, Málaga and La Línea de la Concepción (for Gibraltar). Information on routes and times is available from the local bus companies such as *Transportes Generales Comes* (http://www.tgcomes.es) and *Corporación Española*

The harbour area from the *Puente del Cristo*.

Parador Hotel la Muralla.

de Transporte, CTSA (http://www.ctsa-portillo.com). The nearest airports are Gibraltar Airport (20 km), Jerez Airport (100 km) and Málaga Airport (120 km). You can get a flight to Gibraltar from London, Manchester or Madrid and then take a taxi from the taxi rank in La Línea de la Concepción direct to the ferry terminal in Algeciras. The taxi journey is around thirty minutes and costs about twenty-five euros. To reach the taxi rank, turn right outside the arrivals hall and walk for five minutes to the Spanish frontier (you will need your passport). The taxi rank is on the Spanish side of the frontier. Note: do not go to the taxi rank located immediately outside the airport terminal as this rank serves Gibraltar only and the taxis will not cross the border into Spain.

ACCOMMODATION

Accommodation in Ceuta ranges from four star luxury hotels to budget accommodation at one of the several guesthouses, *hostales*, from around forty euros per night for a double room.

Parador Hotel la Muralla

Paradores de Turismo de España (http://www.parador.es) is a chain of luxury hotels owned by the Spanish government. For around 100 euros a night, a double room at the *Parador Hotel la Muralla* represents good value for those seeking a little bit of luxury. Offers and promotions are often available especially if you are under thirty-five or over fifty-five.

The four star hotel is located in the *Plaza de Nuestra Señora de África*, about ten minutes walk from the ferry terminal and convenient for the centre of Ceuta. Many rooms have sea views. The hotel was built adjacent to the old fortress walls and the original vaults of the old Artillery have been converted into bedrooms. The hotel is modern but with a traditional touch of Moorish and Andalusian features. There is an outdoor swimming pool.

Parador Hotel la Muralla: Some of the bedrooms are converted from the original vaults of the old fortress walls.

Tryp Ceuta

Tryp is a chain of hotels in the *Sol Meliá* group. Located in the *Avenida Alcalde Antonio L. Sánchez Prados*, beside the Municipal Palace, this four star hotel is centrally located and about ten minutes walk from the ferry terminal. There is an outdoor swimming pool.
Website: http://www.solmelia.com

Ulises Hotel

Situated in *Calle Camoens* near the *Plaza de España*, this four star hotel is convenient for the heliport, *Parque Marítimo del Mediterráneo*, shops and city centre. It has a swimming pool.
Website: http://www.hotelulises.com

Hostal Central

On the *Paseo del Revellín*, this guesthouse is in central Ceuta and is convenient for the shops, beach and heliport. Rooms have air conditioning, en suite facilities and WiFi. Single, double, triple and quadruple rooms are available.
Website: http://www.hostalesceuta.com

Hostal Plaza Ruiz

Located near the Hostal Central and under the same management, this guesthouse also offers air conditioning, en suite facilities and WiFi.
Website: http://www.hostalesceuta.com

Murals from the shrine at the *Puente del Cristo*.

EATING OUT

Ceuta has a wide variety of cafes, bars and restaurants ranging from international fast food chains to top-end Spanish restaurants. With a wide range of international cuisine including Moroccan, Italian, Mexican and Chinese restaurants, there is plenty of choice for everyone from the budget traveler to those seeking a culinary experience. Remember that Spanish people do not dine until 8 or 9pm at the earliest and restaurant opening hours reflect this. If you wish to dine out before 8pm you are probably restricted to tapas or a snack in one of the many bars and *cafeterías*, or a burger in McDonalds.

As you would expect from a Mediterranean city, seafood features highly on the city's menus and lovers of seafood will not be disappointed with the range of

Part of the Royal Walls and a view over the rooftops of the city.

fresh fish and shellfish available. Most typical Spanish dishes are widely available while the Moroccan influence contributes excellent kebabs, couscous, mint tea and delicious pastries.

The Chinese restaurant *La Gran Muralla* offers a wide range of traditional Chinese dishes, is centrally located in the *Plaza de la Constitución* and has views over the street and out to sea. The entrance is up some steps off the *Paseo del Revellín*. It is likely to be open slighter earlier in the evening than other restaurants, an important point if you are a visitor used to dining before 9pm. It is an unusual, but not at all unpleasant, experience to eat Chinese food in Spain on the African continent while looking out the window towards the Rock of Gibraltar and the coast of Europe.

Lighter snacks, tapas, pastries and ice cream are widely available in the many bars and *cafeterías*. *El Puente* for example, located in the *Plaza de la Constitución*, serves drinks, snacks and sandwiches. It is modern and trendy with outside seating, ideal for watching the world go by.

SHOPPING

Ceuta does not impose VAT (value added tax) on goods or services. Instead it uses the local I.P.S.I. tax (production, services and import tax), at a much lower tax rate. For this reason many goods are cheaper in Ceuta than in mainland Spain.

The *Mercado Central* off the *Plaza de la Constitución* sells all manner of fresh food including meat, fish, fruit and vegetables. There are also several supermarkets.

The main shopping streets are the *Avenida Alcalde Antonio L. Sánchez Prados*, the *Paseo de Revellín*, the *Calle Camoens*, *Calle Real* and side streets in this area. Fashion shops include Springfield, Zara and Jack and Jones. Due to the low tax situation jewellery shops, perfume shops and designer goods outlets all thrive here.

The *Centro Comercial Parque Ceuta* (Ceuta

The *Casa de los Dragones* in *Calle Camoens*, one of the main shopping streets.

Park Shopping Centre), located in the *Avenida Teniente General Muslera* on the outskirts of the city not far from the port, is a modern shopping centre with supermarkets, shops and cinemas. Department stores in Ceuta include *El Corte Inglés*, one of Spain's main chains of department stores. *El Corte Inglés* is located near the port area.

The *Foso Real* and the Royal Walls.

SIGHTSEEING

The Royal Walls

Construction of the Royal Walls, *Las Muralles Reales*, began in the sixteenth century and was completed during the following two centuries. The fortifications were intended as a defence against attack from the surrounding lands. Begin your visit to the Royal Walls at the bridge, *Puente del Cristo*, over the *Foso Real*. The *Foso Real* is the moat that runs from one side of the isthmus to the other allowing boats to pass from the marina to the bay on the other side. Built during the sixteenth century the moat served as an important defensive feature.

Go through the *Puerta de la Valenciana* (no entrance charge) and you will find yourself in a large parade ground. The Museum of the Royal Walls, *Museo las Murallas Reales*, is located here. This museum houses exhibitions of contemporary art. Admission is free. At the far end of the parade ground there is a gateway leading to the south side of the isthmus.

From the parade ground steps lead up the higher level where there are telescopes and information points and from here you can get a good idea of the various lines of defence formed by the fortifications. There is also a good view over the city, the port and the sea.

On the other side of the moat, the back of the fortifications has vaulted arches which have been converted into bedrooms by the *Hotel Parador La Muralla*. Originally these vaults were used as barracks and military offices.

Part of the Royal Walls of Ceuta.

Parque Marítimo del Mediterráneo

Inside the *Parque Marítimo del Mediterráneo*.

Located off the *Avenue Compañia de Mar*, the Mediterranean Maritime Park, *Parque Marítimo del Mediterráneo*, is a vast complex of artificial salt water lakes, buildings and well-tended gardens designed by César Manrique. Manrique was an artist and architect from Lanzarote in the Canary Islands and the park was the last work he designed before his death. In summer the park serves as a swimming and leisure centre and there is an admission charge. In winter the park is open for walkers and boating on the lakes. Ceuta Casino, a modern building constructed in the style of the Ceuta fortifications, is located in the park, as are several restaurants. There is also a permanent César Manrique exhibition.

Statues and Sculptures

For a city of this size, Ceuta seems to have more than its fair share of statues. Many are of famous Ceutis or were created by local sculptors. A favourite of mine is the one of local doctor and politician, Antonio López Sánchez-Prado, located in the street that bears his name near the Municipal Palace. Someone always seems to ensure that the statue carries fresh flowers in his hand. Another interesting statue is the one of the hooded figure in the *Calle Camoens* representing a member of a Spanish religious order (see page 5).

In the *Plaza de los Reyes* is a modern statue by Ceuti sculptor Elena Laverón, known as the *Monumento a la Convivencia*. It consists of four figures representing Ceuta's main ethnic groups: Christian, Muslim, Jewish and Hindu. Another monument, known as the Monument to Barcelona Football Club, consists of four large pillars representing the four cultures that live in the city. Suspended from the pillars is a sphere representing the world of football. The monument was donated to the city by Barcelona Football Club on the occasion of the 25th World "Trobada" of the Barcelona F.C. Football Association that was held in Ceuta.

A walk along the *Paseo de la Marina Española* not only provides views over the harbour and the *Parque Marítimo del Mediterráneo* but also offers an opportunity to enjoy the many statues and sculptures scattered along this pleasant street.

Look out for the statue of Hercules located on the end of the pier. You can get a good view of this statue from the Algeciras ferry as it passes the entrance to the port.

Antonio López Sánchez-Prado.

The hilltop fortress of Monte Hacho.

An older monument, erected in 1892, located in the *Plaza de África* commemorates the fallen in the African War of 1859-1860. The remains of some of the fallen soldiers are buried here.

Topiary, sculpture created with clipped trees and shrubs, appears to be very popular in Ceuta. Look out for interesting animals and shapes in parks, public spaces and even in the middle of traffic roundabouts.

Almost everywhere you go in Ceuta you will find a statue, sculpture or artwork. They are placed in public squares, parks and gardens and on traffic islands and roundabouts. With many different styles and formats there is something to interest everyone.

Baños Arabes (Arabic Baths)

The ruined remains of an ancient bath house may date from the 11th century, although parts of the building are more likely to have been added in the 14th century. Pieces of marble recovered during excavation are thought to have covered the floors and walls. Located in the *Plaza de la Paz* on the *Paseo de la Marina Española*.

Fortaleza del Hacho

The fort of Monte Hacho overlooks the city from the hilltop. Built at the beginning of the 12th century today a series of walls with semicircular towers still remain, possibly dating from the 16th century. Inside the walls are several 18th century fortresses. As the fort is still used for military purposes tourists are not allowed inside.

Mirador de San Antonio

A converted military battery, this popular viewing point has panoramic views over the strait. On a clear day, you can see the Rock of Gibraltar, the Trafalgar lighthouse in Tarifa, the Yebel Musa Mountain and the nearby town of Castillejos (F'nideq) in Morocco. In spring the setting sun goes down into the sea between the two continents. It is a popular meeting place for young people in the evening.

Topiary is popular in Ceuta.

Dragons adorn the top of the *Casa de los Dragones*.

Nearby is the Monument to the Victory Convoy. This monument, with an image of the Virgin Mary and the footprints of General Franco cast in concrete, commemorates the launch of the Spanish Civil War from the Spanish Territory in Africa in 1936. Created by the local sculptor Bonifacio López Torvizco.

Palacio Municipal

The Municipal Palace, *Palacio Municipal* or *Palacio Asamblea* is the equivalent of the town hall for this autonomous city. It is located beside the Hotel Tryp on the corner of *Avenida Alcalde Antonio L. Sánchez Prados* and the *Plaza de África*. The construction of the Municipal Palace was begun in 1914 on the site of the former town hall and an extension was built in the 1980s in keeping with the old palace. Of note is the imperial staircase, with Portuguese-inspired ceramics, the French-style Throne Room, the Sessions Room and the rotunda.

Ceuta Cathedral

The Cathedral of the Assumption, *Catedral de Santa Maria de la Asunción*, in the *Plaza de África* was built over the site of a mosque that had once been a Byzantine basilica. The current building was completed in 1726 and renovated in the mid 20th century. Of note are the stained glass windows, oil paintings and the side chapel with a baroque altarpiece. The cathedral has a small museum containing various religious artworks, gold artifacts and a 1735 shrine.

Santuario de Nuestra Señora de África

Across the square from the cathedral is the chapel dedicated to the patron saint of Ceuta. The main chapel dates from the 17th century. Of interest are the gilded baroque altarpiece, the gothic *Pietà* of the Virgin Mary erected in 1418 and various 18th century carvings.

Mosque of *Sidi Embarek*

Located on *Calle Claudio Vázquez* this mosque still has an old "*morabito*" or Muslim convent possibly dating from the 18th century. There is a Muslim cemetery nearby. The mosque has been extensively restored in recent decades. Entrance to the mosque is restricted to Muslim worshippers.

Ceuta cathedral.

Synagogue of *Bet-El*

Built in the 1970s to replace and modernize the old synagogue in Ceuta. Of interest are the brightly coloured stained-glass windows and the general layout of the room.

MUSEUMS

There are nine small museums in Ceuta. Three of these are military museums reflecting Ceuta's origins as a fortified city. Most of the museums and exhibitions are free to enter, a happy situation that encourages tourists and locals to pop in even if only for a few minutes when time is short. For opening times you should check locally with the tourist office or online at http://www.ceuta.es.

Ancient map of the Mediterranean Sea showing the location of Ceuta.

Ceuta Museum

Conveniently located on the *Paseo de Revellín*, one of the main shopping streets, the building was built in 1900 as a military barracks and was formerly home to Spanish soldiers, amongst them Francisco Franco. Its rooms are dedicated to ancient, medieval, modern and contemporary history cataloguing Ceuta's past from prehistoric times through to the present day. Temporary painting and photography exhibitions are also housed in the museum. Free entrance.

The Museum of the Royal Walls

On the *Avenida San Francisco Javier*, with its entrance located within the parade ground, the *Museo las Murallas Reales* houses temporary exhibitions of contemporary art. Admission is free.

Exposición Permanente César Manrique

On the *Avenida Compañía de Mar*, entrance from within the *Parque Marítimo del Mediterráneo*, this small permanent photography exhibition highlights the work of the Canary Island artist, César Manrique, the designer and creator of the Maritime Park.

"*El Desnarigado*" Military Museum

The *Museo Militar* on the *Carretera del Desnarigado* owes its name to a Berber pirate nicknamed "*el desnarigado*" (flat-nosed), who escaped from an

Detail of a mural.

Algerian prison-mine and settled here in 1417. The museum is dedicated to the history of the various weapons and military forces of Ceuta and houses weapons and uniforms from the 16th to the 19th century. Entrance is free.

The Museum of the Legion

The *Museo Específico de La Legión* on the *Paseo Colón* catalogues the history of the Spanish Foreign Legion from its founding in 1920 to the present day. Founded in 1940, the collection was moved from Dar-Riffien (Morocco) to its current location in 1978. There is no entrance charge.

The Army Museum

The *Museo Específico de Regulares* is the museum of the regular army in Ceuta (as opposed to the Foreign Legion). It is located in the army barracks in *Calle Claudio Vázquez* and admission is free.

Maritime Museum

The *Fundación Museo del Mar* on the *Muelle de España* (the port area) is dedicated to the marine port and maritime history of Ceuta. It contains a permanent exhibition showing the development of the port from the 19th century to the present day. It also houses temporary exhibitions and is used as a venue for conventions and conferences. There is no admission fee but visits are by prior appointment only.

Cathedral Museum

The cathedral in the *Plaza de África* has a small museum. The *Museo y Archivo Catedralicio* contains religious pictures, gold and silver objects, books and vestments from the 15th to the 20th century. Free admission.

Basilica Museum

The *Museo de la Basílica Tardorromana de Ceuta* is located on *Calle Queipo de Llano* on the site of the Roman basilica dating from the middle of the 4th century. The exhibits are mainly recent archaeological findings that portray the history of Ceuta. Free admission.

Ceuta Cathedral in the Plaza de África.

BEACHES

Ceuta has around twenty one kilometres of coastline including several pleasant beaches, coves and bays. The beaches are within easy reach of the city centre and you can choose from the Atlantic coast to the north, or the Mediterranean coast to the south. The locals advise that the water is colder and rougher on the northern coast compared to the warmer, calmer water of the Mediterranean.

A view of the cathedral from the *La Ribera* beach.

La Ribera

Along the *Calle Independencia*, just minutes from the *Plaza de África*, this south-facing beach has fine white sand and all the modern amenities you would expect from a beach that has gained the European Blue Flag award.

El Chorrillo

Further westwards on the southern coast is the sandy *Playa El Chorrillo*, with similar amenities. At the end of *El Chorrillo* beach there are several coves in the *Almadraba* area. These are popular with locals and fishermen.

Playa Benítez

Consisting mainly of pebbles, this beach is on the Atlantic coast about 600 metres west of the port area. This beach is popular with water-sport enthusiasts and local residents.

Playa de Benzú

Further along the Atlantic coast, near the border with Morocco, this gravel beach is small and visited mainly by local residents. It is also popular with scuba divers and for watching sunsets.

There are several other small beaches and rocky coves on both coasts. Some can only be accessed by foot.

Calle Independencia with *Playa de la Ribera* on the right.

SPORTS AND ACTIVITIES

Kayak Hire

Sea canoe trips for all age groups are available from April to September from *La Ribera* Beach. As well as admiring the picturesque coastline you may spot sea turtles or dolphins.

Horse Riding

Two separate riding schools offer classical riding, rodeo-style riding, different levels of training and treks along the mountain paths that surround the city.

Club Náutico

The Ceuta Yacht Club is located in the marina area, the *Dársena Deportiva*. It offers courses in sailing, canoeing, fishing and underwater activities.

Scuba Diving

The Strait of Gibraltar is a regular migration path for numerous marine species creating a diversity and wealth of underwater flora and fauna. Ceuta is widely recognized as an ideal site for underwater exploration and offers a wide variety of diving sites. In the 8 to 10 metre dive sites you can spot pollack, forkbeard, bream, grouper, octopus and large pelagic fish. At 20 to 30 metres you can find spider crabs and artificial reefs created by sunken rafts; deeper still you can find rare species such as red coral. There are several diving clubs in Ceuta.

Hill Walking, Hiking or Rambling

Known as "*senderismo*" in Spanish there is a local group, AVISCE (*Asociación Virtual de Senderistas de Ceuta*), that promotes this activity in Ceuta. They can advise you on paths and routes in the countryside on the outskirts of the city. The website is at http://www.avisce.es.vg

Motor Sports

Ceuta offers activities for quad bikes, scrambler bikes, trial bikes and 4x4s. A local club, the Africa Star 4x4 Adventure Sports Club of Ceuta (http://www.africastar4x4.com), organizes guided trips on off-road routes.

A view southwards from the Calle Independencia.

Club Náutico de Ceuta.

Fishing

Deep-sea fishing from a boat provides the opportunity to catch tuna, sama fish and squid. Ceuta has many popular places for fishing from the coast or beach where you can catch many varieties of fish including gilthead bream and sea bass. There are several fishing clubs.

A view southwards from *La Ribera* beach; the coast of Morocco is in the distance.

FIESTAS AND EVENTS

Los Reyes Magos

Celebrated on January 6th, this is the last of the Christmas celebrations. There is a cavalcade of the Three Kings and traditional cakes, *roscones*, are available in the local pastry shops.

Ceuta Carnival

Held in February or March, this involves a colourful procession through the streets, with floats, masks and costumes. There is live music and the highlight of the carnival is a ceremony known as the "Burial of the Mackerel".

Easter and Holy Week

The thirteen brotherhoods of Ceuta and the local convents do penitence through the city. Religious images and banners are carried through the streets. In the evening the tapas bars are busy.

May Crosses

The arrival of spring is celebrated with decorative flowers and there is a competition for the best "May Cross".

Corpus Christi

The royal banner of Ceuta is carried in a procession through the streets. Religious, civil and military authorities take part.

Romería de San Antonio

Held on June 13th, Saint Antony's day, the tradition of this popular fiesta goes back to Portuguese times.

Playas de Ceuta.

A view northwards over the marina; the hill of Monte Hacho is visible on the right of the picture.

An image of the saint is carried in procession from the hermitage of San Antonio, on Monte Hacho. According to legend, young people looking for love should sit on the altar's steps.

Nuestra Señora del Carmen

Celebrated on June 16th, this festival is related to the sea and is particularly popular with fishermen and seafarers. There are two processions and the fishermen place a statue of *Nuestra Señora del Carmen* in a small decorated boat at the port entrance.

Hogueras de San Juan

This festival takes place on June 24th, Saint John's day, although it also claims pagan origins. This very popular festival celebrates the shortest night of the year with concerts, bonfires and fireworks on the city beaches. It is reputedly lucky to swim in the sea at midnight.

Fiestas Patronales

Celebrated on August 5th, this festival honours the patron saint of the city, *Nuestra Señora de África*. On the previous day, bunches of flowers are taken to *Plaza de África* to be offered to the Virgin. On August 5th, a statue of the Virgin is taken in procession and flowers are thrown down from the balconies of the city. Ceuta Fair, which begins at the end of July and is held in the *Paseo de la Marina Española*, has its grand finale on this day.

Ceuta Day

September 2nd is the official holiday of Ceuta. On this day in 1415 Juan I of Portugal left Ceuta and gave control to D. Pedro de Meneses.

San Daniel y Compañeros Mártires

On October 10th there are religious and general celebrations in remembrance of the seven Franciscan monks martyred in Ceuta on the 10th of October, 1227.

The Rock of Gibraltar.

Rucksack Day

Rucksack Day, *Día de la Mochila*, is held on November 1st, All Saints Day. The tradition in Ceuta is to spend a day in the countryside, taking a rucksack with sandwiches, fruit and nuts. The origin of the custom is from the Spanish practice of visiting cemeteries on this day in order to place flowers on the graves of deceased relatives and remain there all day. Many locals camp out the previous night in the country areas outside the city. One of the popular areas is the *Cala del Desnarigado*.

A view from the Rock of Gibraltar looking towards Algeciras. Gibraltar town and port area are in the foreground; the airport runway can be seen jutting out into the bay. Beyond the runway are the marina and town of La Línea de la Concepción.

EXCURSIONS

Excursion to Gibraltar

If Ceuta is a piece of Spain in Africa, then Gibraltar is a piece of Great Britain in Spain. A British colony for the last 300 years, Gibraltar is described as a self-governing British overseas territory (http://www.gibraltar.gi). Less than two hours travelling time from Ceuta, Gibraltar makes an interesting and enjoyable day trip. It involves travelling between Spain and Great Britain and indeed between the African continent and Europe, so remember to take your passport. English is the official language of Gibraltar although most people also speak Spanish. Drive on the right-hand side of the road, not on the left as in the UK. You do not need to change your watch as Gibraltar is in the same time zone as Spain. The currency is the Gibraltar pound, which is identical in value to a pound sterling. British pounds are also legal tender here. Gibraltar pounds are not legal tender in the UK but can be swapped for British pounds in a bank. The euro is widely accepted but you will not get a good rate of exchange from shops or taxi drivers.

To travel to Gibraltar from Ceuta you need to take one of the numerous fast-ferries to Algeciras. Crossing the Strait of Gibraltar takes less than an hour and offers some panoramic views of the Rock of Gibraltar as well as the North African coast. There is a taxi rank at the ferry terminal in Algeciras. The Spanish taxis will not go into Gibraltar but will take you to the border. The town on the Spanish side of the border is called La Línea de

A Barbary Ape in Gibraltar.

The Rock of Gibraltar.

la Concepción or simply La Línea. Ask the driver for *La Línea cerca de la frontera*. The taxi fare is around 25 euros and the journey takes about 30 minutes. The taxi will take you to the border checkpoint where you simple walk through the pedestrian channel showing your passport and then proceed through customs. This process takes only a few minutes in stark contrast to the vehicle channel where queues of three hours are not uncommon in busy periods. A few minutes walk from the checkpoint brings you to the airport terminal.

The airport in Gibraltar is unique. The ageing terminal has a beautiful faded elegance and the coffee shop upstairs has great views of the Rock. The runway was built laterally across the peninsula – the only way they could fit it in – and runs from the beach on one side all the way to the sea on the other side. In order to have a sufficiently long runway there was no room for the main road that links the Spanish border to central Gibraltar. To solve this problem the main road crosses the runway, with a set of traffic lights to stop the traffic and pedestrians when a plane is landing or taking off. This system works well as there are currently only a few flights per day. Gibraltar hopes to expand the number of flights and an expensive new terminal is being constructed with plans to re-route the road.

To get to central Gibraltar take bus number 3 from the airport. This bus goes all the way to Europa Point but you should get off at the cinema. This is very near the lower station of the cable car – the best way to travel to the top of the Rock. You can also walk the kilometre into town or take a taxi. Gibraltar taxi drivers do a very hard sell on the official "Rock Tour", a tour of the major sights by taxi or minibus for a minimum of four people that takes about 90 minutes. However, as Gibraltar is less than seven square kilometres, it is much cheaper and, in my opinion, more rewarding to get around on foot or by using the efficient public bus system.

Gibraltar is a lovely quirky mixture of Britain and Spain complete with helmeted policemen, double-decker buses and pints of beer, all overlaid with a Mediterranean sunshine and tempered by an Andalusian cuisine. Enjoy a pint of beer in the sunshine, while away some time in the botanic gardens and take the cable car to the top of the rock. The views from the top are stunning and you will almost certainly see the famous Barbary Apes. To be scientifically correct they are Barbary Macaques and are monkeys rather than apes but in Gibraltar everyone calls them apes. Apart

A Barbary Ape sits by the roadside.

from humans they are the only primates that live freely in Europe.

Although Gibraltar has one of the lowest crime rates in Europe these statistics refer only to human criminals. The rock apes will steal your lunch, camera, purse, or anything else you possess, so be careful. They are adept at opening bags. Remember also that although they show no fear of humans and look particularly cute, they are wild animals and can bite.

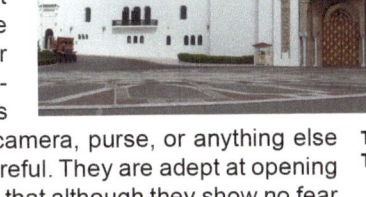

The Royal Palace in Tetuan.

Excursion to Tetuan

If you have a day to spare, or even half a day, you can travel to Tetuan and experience the sights, tastes and smells of Morocco, or *Marruecos* in Spanish. Tetuan is only 40 kilometres to the south of Ceuta and is one of the nearest towns. Declared "Heritage of Mankind" by the United Nations, Tetuan is well worth a visit although getting there requires overcoming some minor obstacles. Because Ceuta is in Spain and therefore in Europe (at least politically if not geographically) travelling from Ceuta to Tetuan not only involves travelling from one country to another, but also from one continent to another. You will need a valid passport and possibly a visa. EU citizens do not normally require a visa.

There is no bus or train that runs between Ceuta and Morocco and neither Spanish nor Moroccan taxi drivers will cross the border. It is necessary therefore to travel to the border post at El Tarajal, walk through the crossing and take a taxi on the Moroccan side.

Bus number 7 runs from central Ceuta to the border and takes about 15 minutes. Catch the bus at *Plaza de la Constitución* on the street outside the covered market, *el Mercado Central* and ask for a ticket to *la frontera*. It costs less than a euro. *La frontera* is the terminus; the bus stops there and then returns to central Ceuta.

Remember that Morocco uses dirhams as currency although most taxi drivers and traders will welcome euros. It is worth having some dirhams as the exchange rate you get in a bank is more favourable. If you have not already changed your money there is a foreign exchange kiosk on the Spanish side of the border near the bus stop. Remember also

Church in Tetuan.

Mosque in Tetuan.

that Morocco is in a different time zone, one hour behind Spanish time. Don't forget to change your watch.

When you arrive at the border you will notice a more North African atmosphere compared to central Ceuta. Go through the pedestrian checkpoint where Spanish customs officials will inspect your passport. You will then find yourself in a "no-man's-land" between Europe and Africa. You must obtain a white form to complete with your personal details, passport number, etc. This is a small, postcard sized form in Arabic and French but it is fairly obvious where to write your name, passport number, etc. Take this to be signed at the police window and put the form in your passport. The passport and signed form must be presented at the Moroccan border post. You are then permitted to proceed through the checkpoint and you officially enter Africa.

In this "no-man's-land" there are numerous people that will offer you help and advice. These are not officials. Some are simply hoping for a small tip and may be helpful while some may be less salubrious. Judge for yourself.

On the return trip the procedure is simply reversed. You need a yellow form instead of a white one. The bus back to the centre of Ceuta will stop on the opposite side of the road to where it dropped you.

Once through to the Moroccan side of the border you will be faced with an array of white taxis and local people wanting to act as your "guide". Some of these appear to be official guides complete with photographic ID. Choose for yourself. You do not need a guide but a guide will take you to places in

Donkeys are still used for transport in the narrow streets of the *medina*.

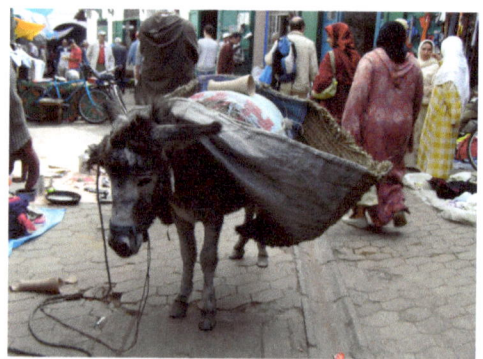

the *souk* and *kasbah* that you would never find on your own. If you do accept the services of a guide it is advisable to agree in advance for how long you want his services and how much to pay. A guide will probably save you money by negotiating a taxi fare for you, almost certainly lower than you would be able to do on your own. In Morocco, always negotiate the fare before you get into the taxi.

The taxi ride to Tetuan will take about 40 minutes and cost around 10 to 15 euros (at the time of writing about 100 to 150 dirhams). The road is relatively good, which is more than can be said of the taxis. These tend to be old and in poor mechanical order. Do not expect seat belts.

In Tetuan, stop for a well-earned cup of mint tea, it is surprisingly refreshing. Do not ask for beer or wine, Morocco is predominantly a Muslim country and alcohol is not usually available.

A typical shop in the *souk*.

Tetuan is a city of two parts; the "new city" is modern with streets that are fairly wide and straight. The main street is Mohammed V Avenue and here you will find shops and cafes. The Archaeological museum is located at the end of the street in Al Yalaa square. The Royal Palace is situated in Hassan II Square. An impressive building but unfortunately not open to the public. This is also where the new city meets the old city.

The *medina* or "old city" contains many very narrow and maze-like streets, houses, workshops, stalls and mosques. Craftsmen such as weavers, jewellers and leather workers will be happy to sell you a souvenir. The *souk* is the market area within the *medina* and you will encounter a heady mixture of aromas from the stalls selling spices, meat, vegetables, livestock and fish. Remember every price is negotiable and the price you are first quoted may well be many times more than the vendor expects to receive. Carpet salesmen are particularly adept at extracting money from tourists. Do not buy anything you don't want or at any rate do not pay more than its worth, but have fun looking and haggling.

A view over the rooftops of the old city with the Rif Mountains in the background.

To the south of the city you gain a good view of the Rif Mountains. Finish your visit with a typical Moroccan meal of lamb *shish kebab* served with *couscous* and of course a glass of mint tea. Vegetarians can ask for a vegetable *couscous*.

The flag of Ceuta.

CEUTA FACTS AND FIGURES

Time zone: CET (GMT+1h) and CEST (GMT+2h) in summer
Size: 23 square kilometres
Population: around 77,000
Official currency: Euro
Official language: Spanish
Post code: 51000
Telephone prefix: 956
Business hours:
    Monday to Friday: 10am to 2pm and 5 to 9pm
    Saturday: 10 am to 2 pm
Climate
    Average temperature: 18° C
    Average high: 19° C
    Average low: 16° C
    Maximum temperature: 33 °C
    Minimum temperature: 7 °C
    Days of sun: 300
    Days of rain: 40
Post Office (*Correos*): *Plaza de España*
Police Station: *Avenida de España*
Tourist Offices:
- Main office
    Oficina de Turismo
    Baluarte de los Mallorquines
    Calle Edrissis, s/n.
    Baluarte de los Mallorquines
    Tel: (0034) 856 200 560
    Fax: (0034) 856 200 565
    email: turismo@ceuta.es
- Ferry terminal (ground floor)
    Oficina de Turismo
    Estación Marítima de Ceuta
    Avda. Muelle Cañonero Dato, s/n.
    Tel: (0034) 956 506 275

HINTS AND TIPS

- Get a free map of Ceuta from the Tourist Office before you go (address above). They also supply brochures, leaflets and booklets, available in both Spanish and English.
- Visit the tourist office when you arrive. They are very helpful and will provide up-to-date information on opening times, local events, ferry times, local buses and much more.
- Learn some Spanish or bring a phrase book. Ceuta is a popular destination for Spanish tourists but waiters are not yet used to the English-speaking tourists.
- Use local buses; there is a good service and reasonably cheap.
- At the ferry port, remember to exchange your ticket for a boarding card. You must do this before you go through security.
- Many Moroccan restaurants and bars in Ceuta do not serve alcohol.
- Remember that in Ceuta you need euros; in Morocco, dirhams; in Gibraltar, pounds. You can use euros in all three places but may get a very bad rate of exchange.
- You will need your passport for any trips outside Ceuta, for example Morocco, Spain, Gibraltar.
- If you visit Gibraltar, remember that although it has one of the lowest crime rates in Europe, they are only referring to crimes committed by humans. The monkeys will steal anything that's not nailed down, especially food, cameras and bags.

The coat of arms of Ceuta.

USEFUL WEB SITES

Tourist Information
- www.ceuta.es   Official information site of the autonomous city. In Spanish, English and French
- www.spain.info/ven/provincias/ceuta.html   Official site of the *Instituto de Turismo de España* (*TURESPAÑA*)
- www.avisce.es.vg   Asociacion Virtual de Senderistas de Ceuta
- www.africastar4x4.com   Motor sport in Ceuta

Helicopter Ceuta/Málaga
- www.grupoinaer.com/index.php?/inaer/malagaceuta
- www.edreams.com/flights/malaga-ceuta

Ferry Ceuta/Algeciras
- www.trasmediterranea.es
- www.euroferrys.com
- www.balearia.com

Spanish Railways
- www.renfe.es
- www.spanish-rail.co.uk

Bus Companies in Southern Spain
- www.tgcomes.es
- www.ctsa-portillo.com

Ceuta Hotels
- www.parador.es
- www.booking.com/ceuta
- www.hostalesceuta.com
- www.solmelia.com
- www.hotelulises.com

Gibraltar Tourism
- www.gibraltar.gi

Morocco Tourism
- www.visitmorocco.com

Publisher of Ceuta Mini Guide
- www.savannapress.com

The Spanish flag flies over all public buildings in Ceuta.

The arab influence can be seen in the style and decor of many buildings in Ceuta.

FEEDBACK REQUEST

We very much welcome feedback from our readers. Please contact us if you can provide any new or updated information relating to any topic covered by this book, or if you would like to send us any comments or suggestions for improvement. In particular we welcome:

- Notification of any errors in the book

- Notification of any outdated or incorrect information

- Updated information on any topic covered in this book

- New information that you feel should be in the book

- Hints or tips on any aspect of the destinations featured in this book

- Suggestions for improvements to the book

- Any comments, good or bad, about the book

Your suggestions will help us compile a new edition and ensure that we provide useful and up-to-date information. Please contact us at:

www.savannapress.com

View from Ceuta.

www.ingramcontent.com/pod-product-compliance
Lightning Source LLC
Chambersburg PA
CBHW042045290426
44109CB00001B/39